# SCHIRMER'S LIBRARY
## OF MUSICAL CLASSICS

T0071669

Vol. 1750

# HENRY SCHRADIECK

## The School of Violin-Technics

### Book I

Transcribed for the

# Viola

by

SAMUEL LIFSCHEY

# G. SCHIRMER, Inc.

DISTRIBUTED BY

HAL•LEONARD®
CORPORATION
7777 W. BLUEMOUND RD. P.O. BOX 13819 MILWAUKEE, WI 53213

# The School of Violin-Technics
## Book I
### Exercises for promoting dexterity in the various positions

**Explanation of the signs**

I   A String
II  D String
III G String
IV  C String

remain—Stay in given position until a fingering
indicates change of position

Henry Schradieck
Edited for Viola by
Samuel Lifschey

## I
### Exercises on One String

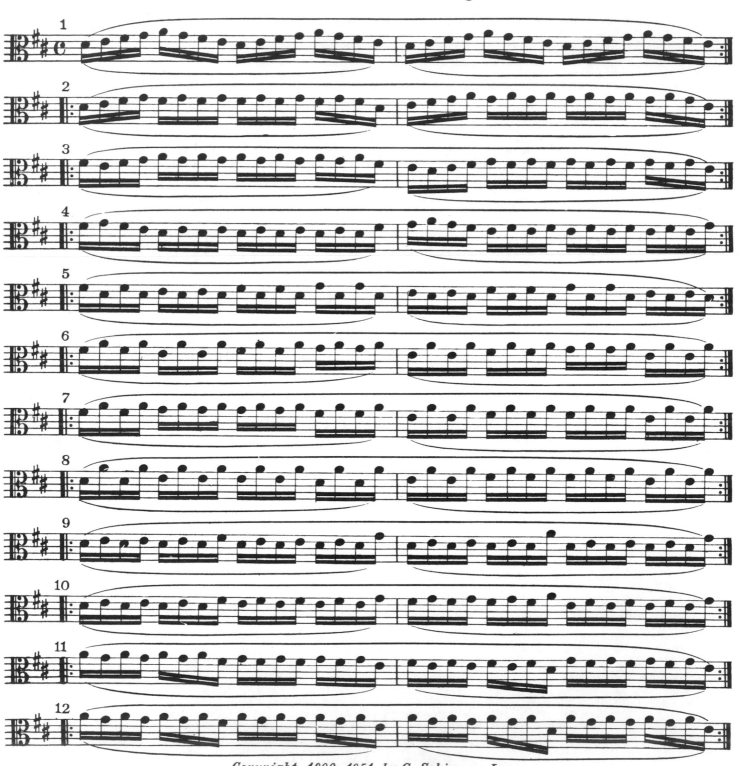

Copyright, 1900, 1951, by G. Schirmer, Inc.
Copyright renewed, 1927
Renewal Copyright assigned to G. Schirmer, Inc.
Printed in the U.S.A.

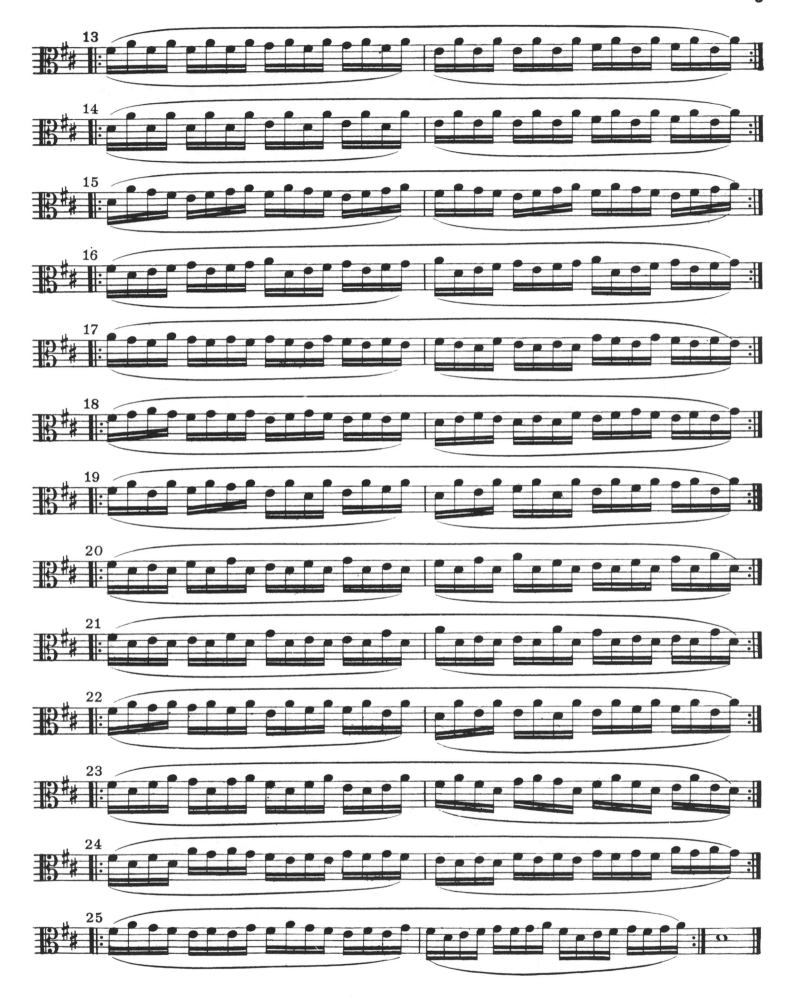

*) If this fourth-finger extension is not feasible at this stage, the small note may be substituted.

# III
## Exercises on Two Strings

# IV

Exercises to be practiced with wrist movement only, keeping the right arm perfectly quiet

# V
## Exercises on Three Strings

## Exercises on Four Strings

retain fingers on string wherever possible

retain the first finger

## Exercises in the Second Position

# IX

## Exercises in the First and Second Positions

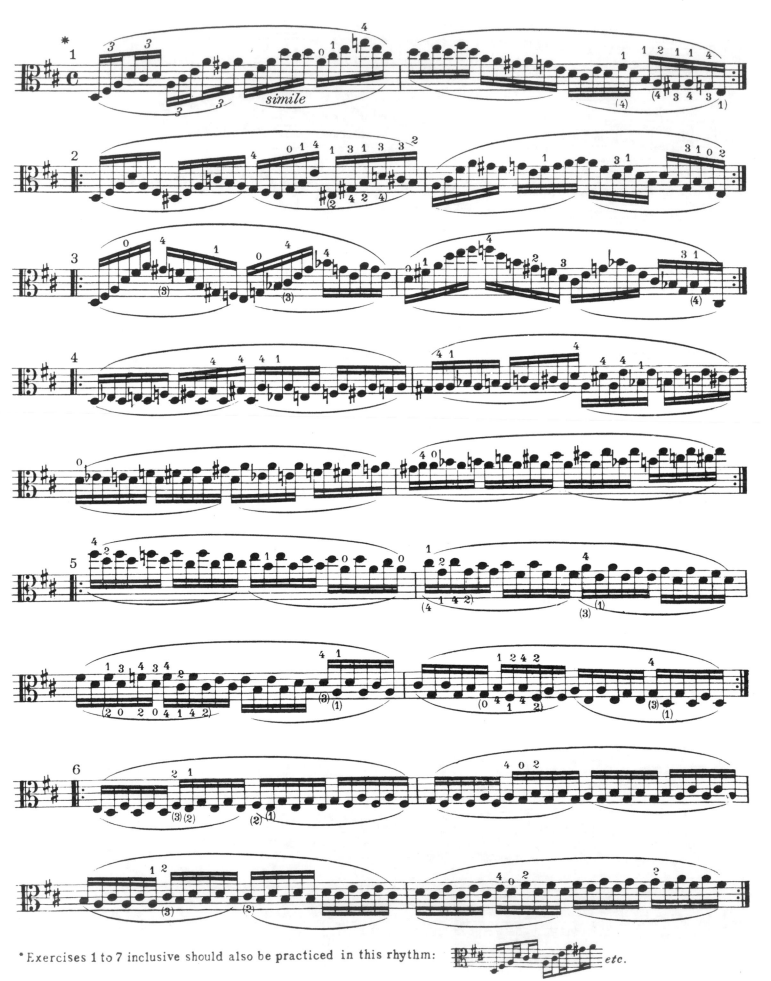

* Exercises 1 to 7 inclusive should also be practiced in this rhythm: etc.

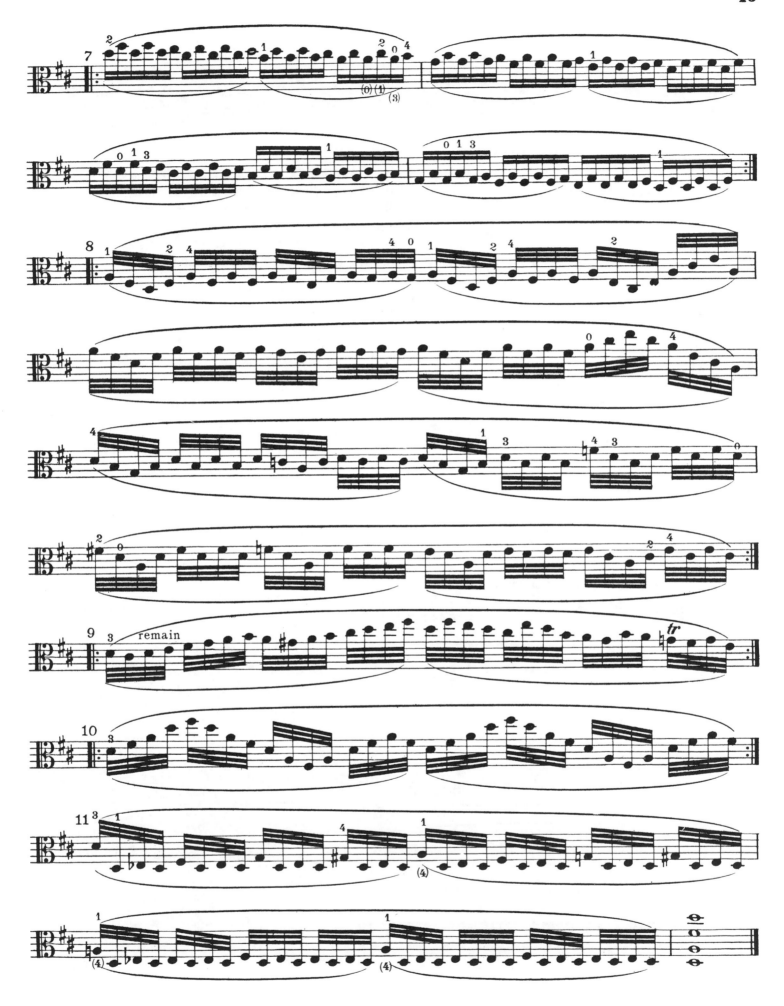

# X
## Exercises in the Third Position

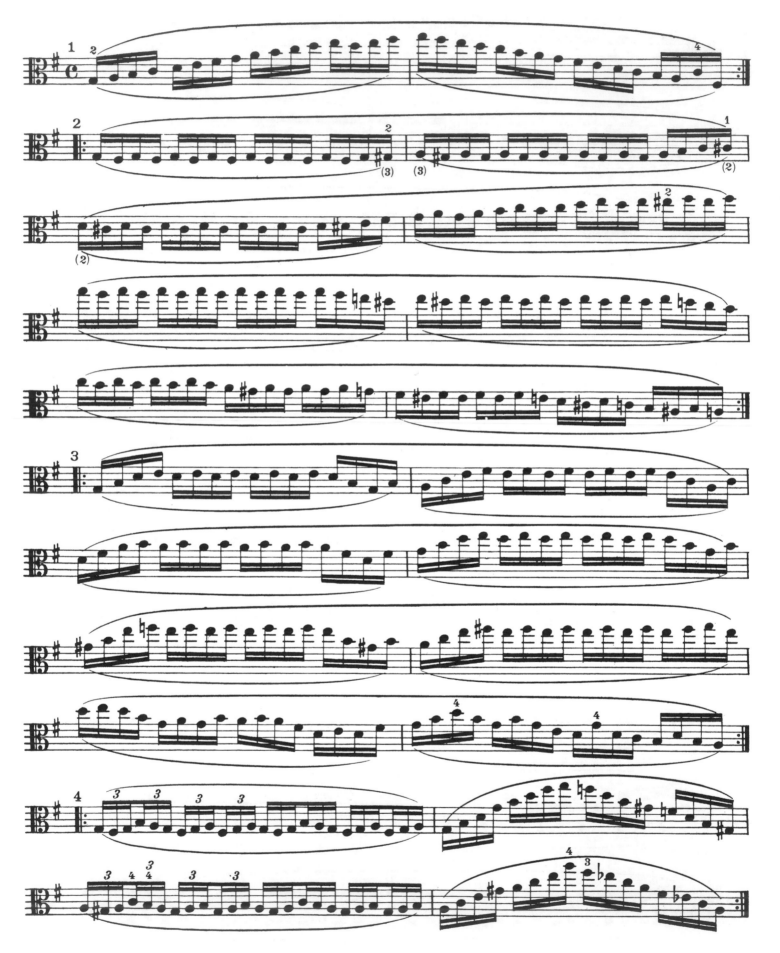

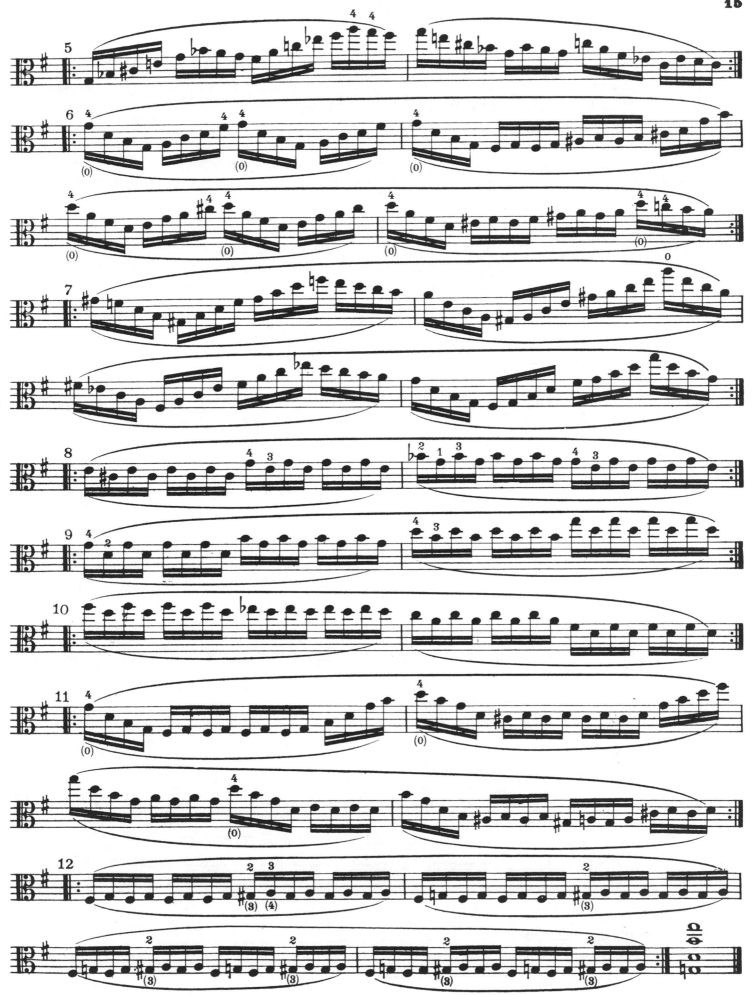

# XI
## Exercises in the First, Second, and Third Positions

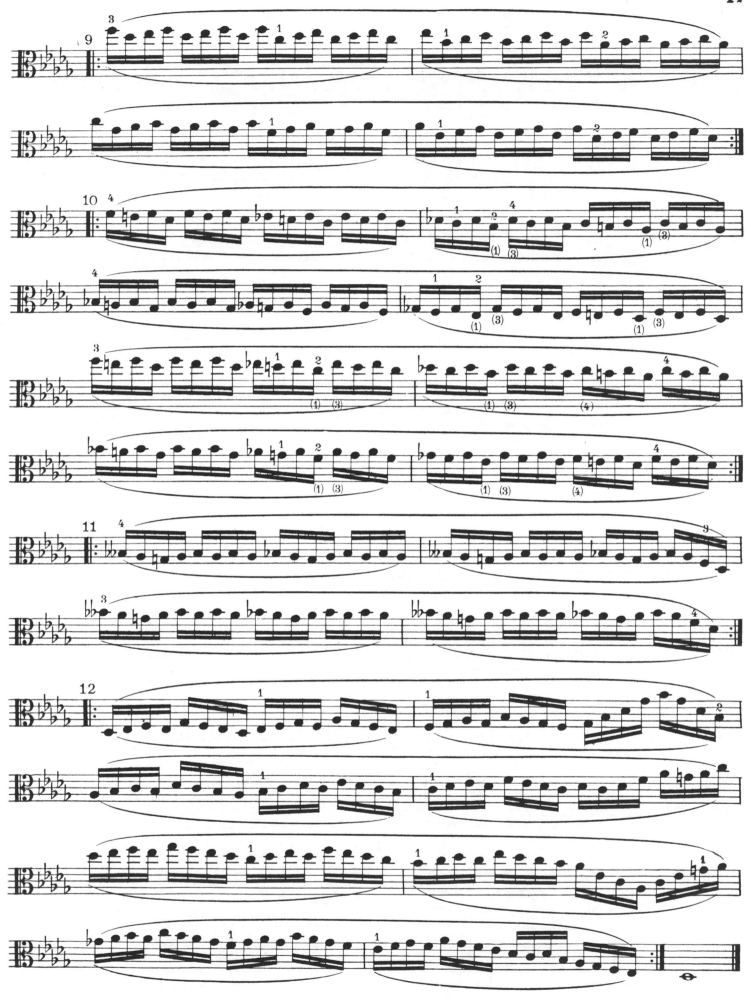

# XII
## Exercises in the Fourth Position

# XIII
## Exercises in the First, Second, Third, and Fourth Positions

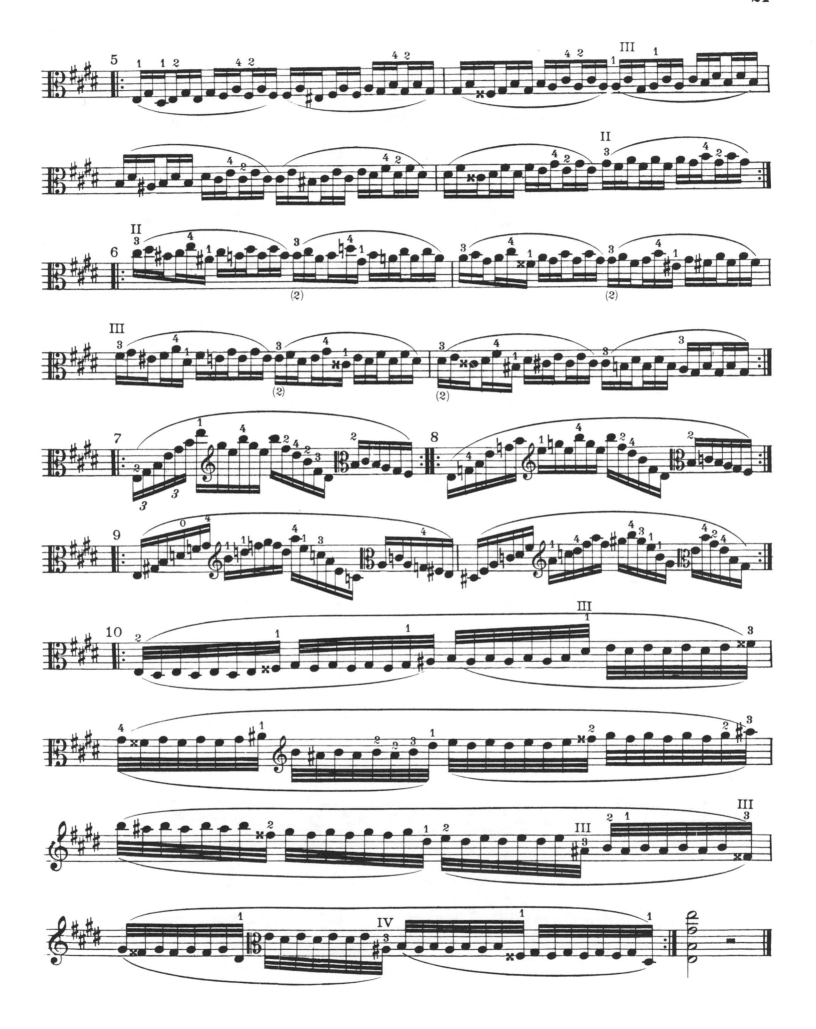

# XIV
## Exercises in the Fifth Position

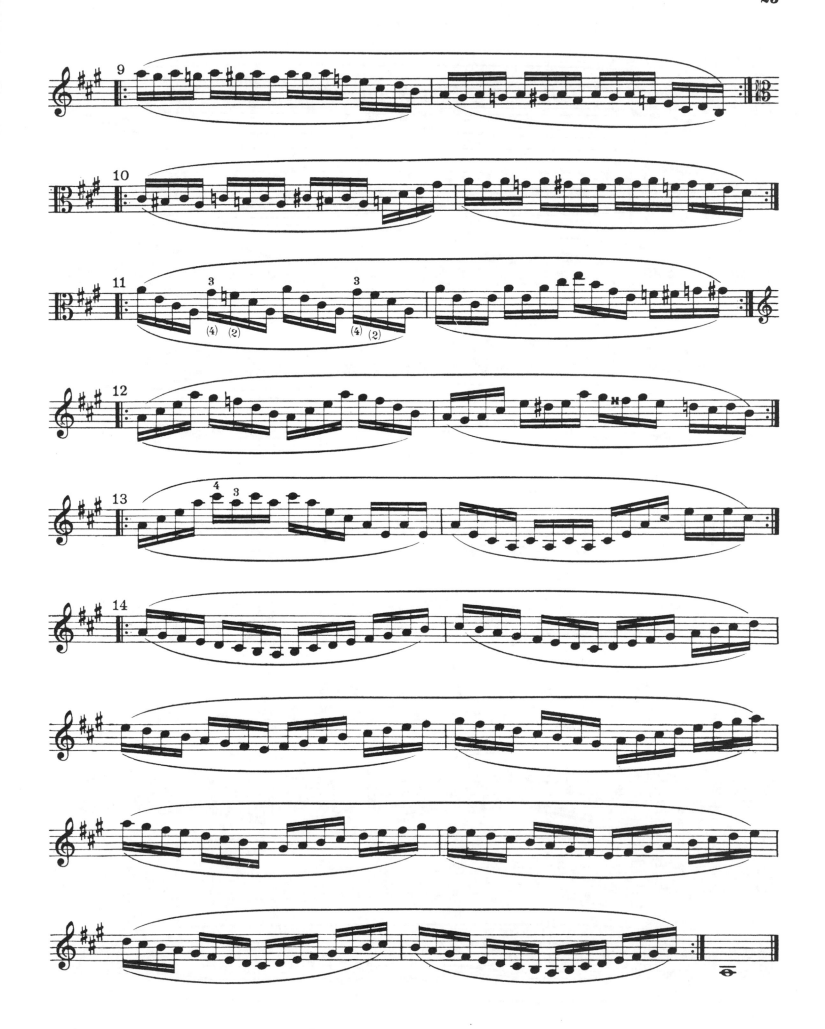

# XV
## Exercises passing through the first Five Positions

# XVI
## Exercises in the Sixth Position

Because of the greatly increased space between the strings and fingerboard in this register, and the resulting awkward and possibly distorted position of the left hand and arm (especially when playing on a wide viola), fatigue and cramp may well ensue. When this occurs, the player is strongly advised to rest until all sensations of fatigue and cramp disappear.

# XVII
## Exercises passing through the first Six Positions

# XVIII
## Exercises in the Seventh Position
### cf. Note on page 26, Exercise XVI

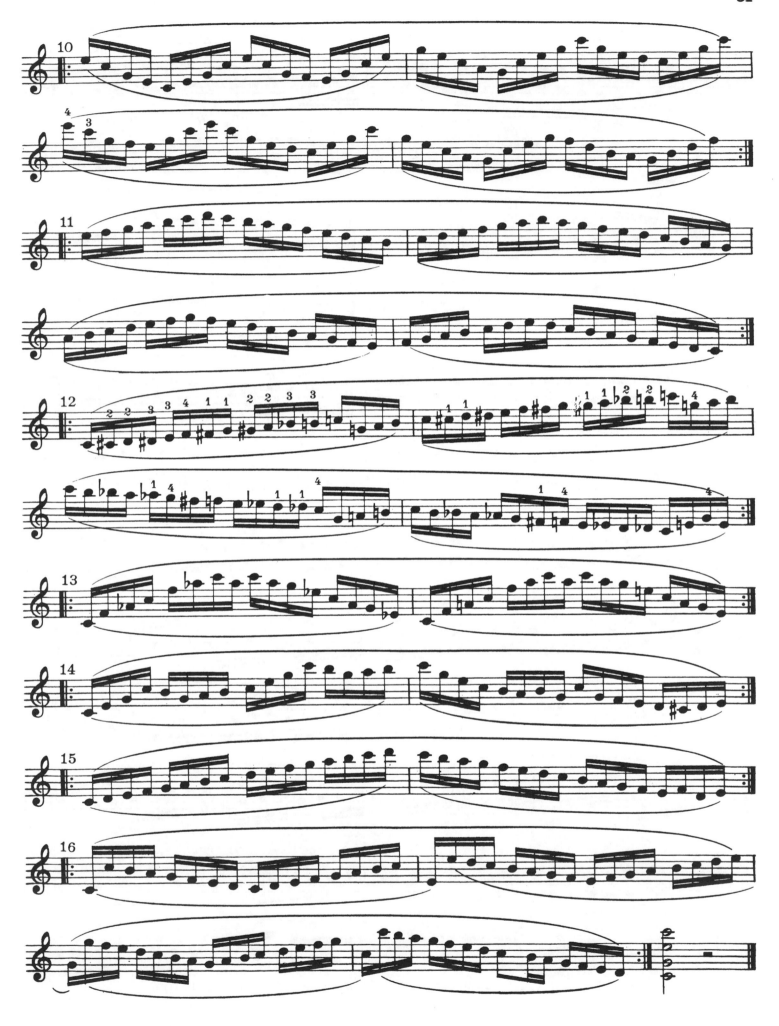

# XIX

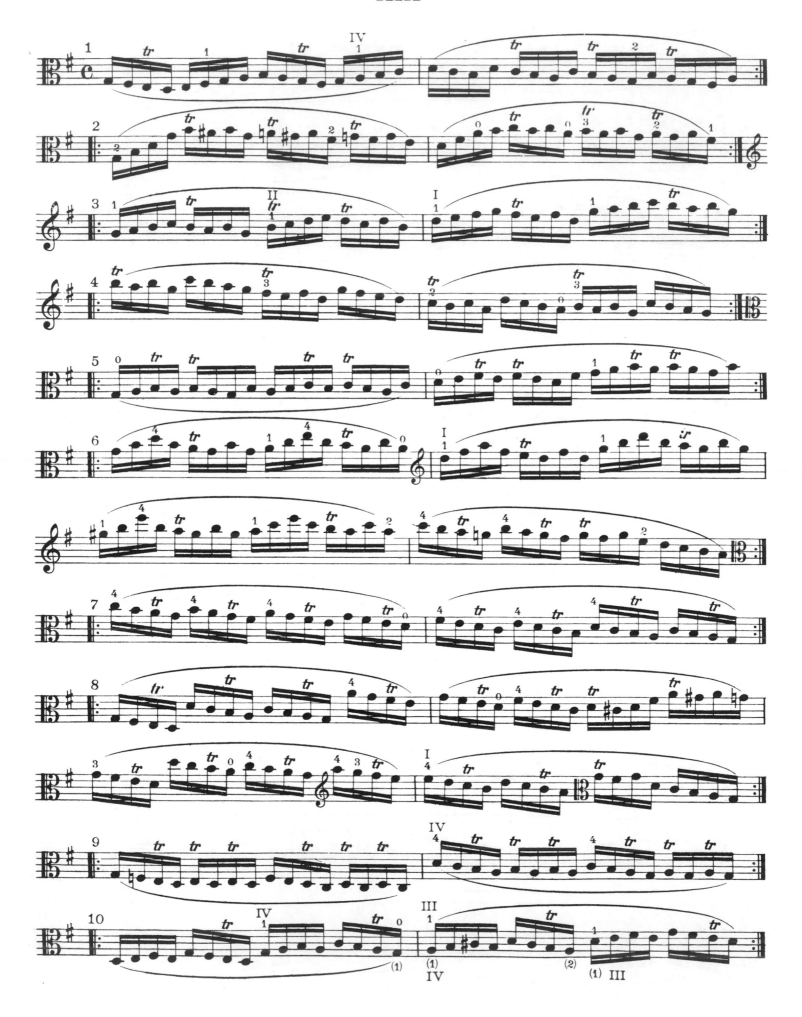

# XX

Allegro

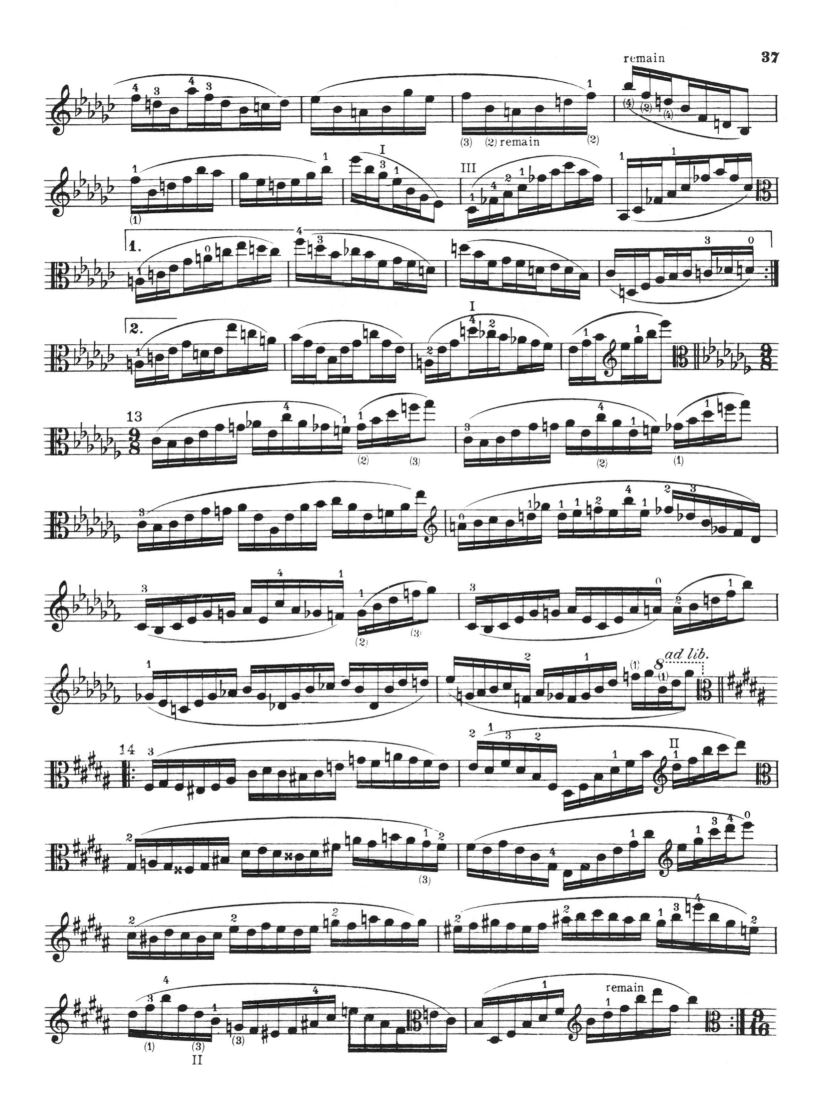

Allegro vivace

Energico

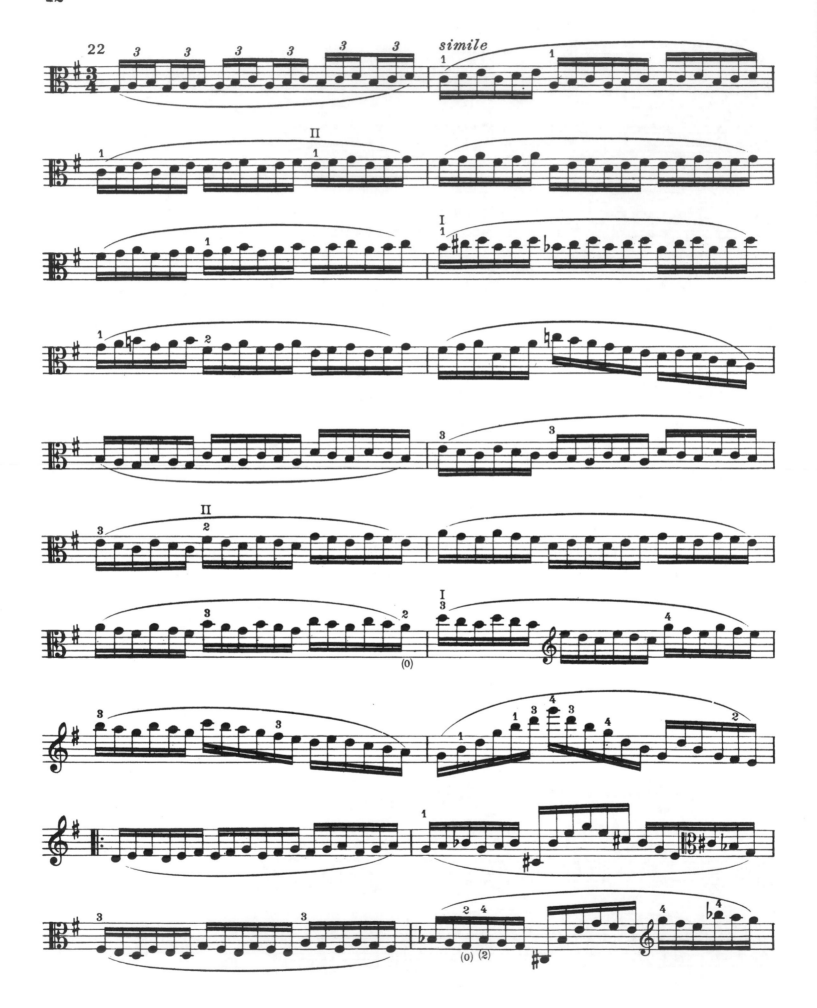

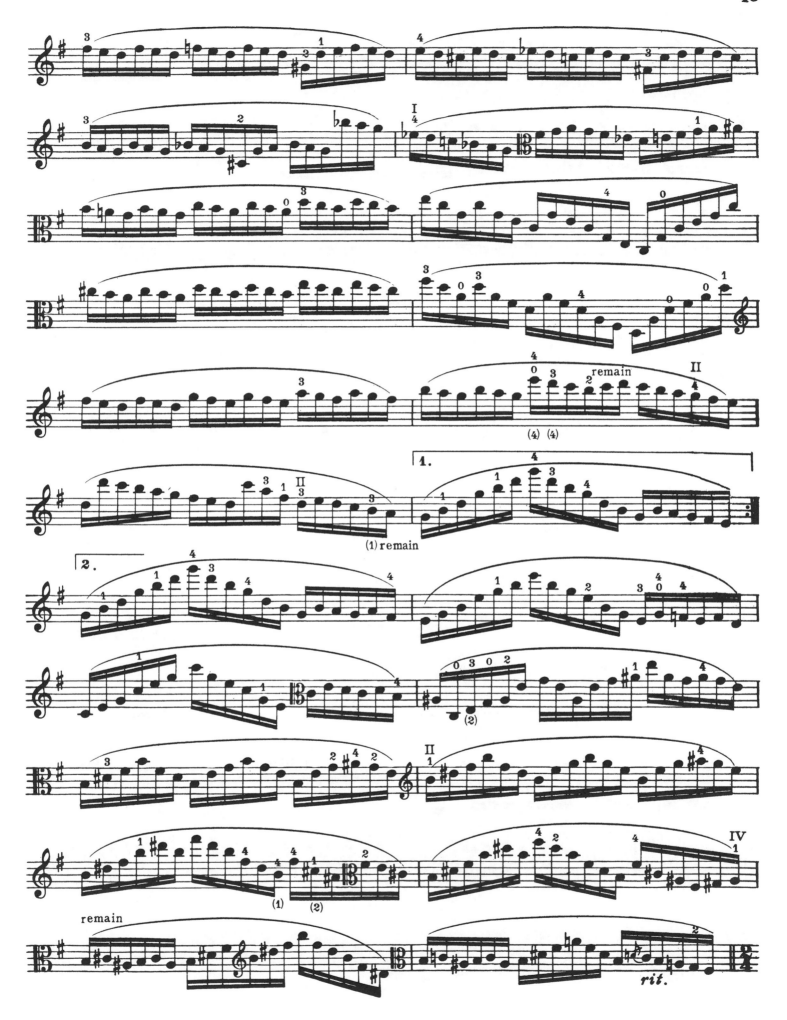

at the middle of the bow

25

a tempo

26

rit.